Manx Car Races
The Golden Years
1904–1953
VOLUME ONE

Photo: Three times holder of the World Land Speed Record, Capt. George Eyston also raced motorcycles and cars. He finished third in the 1934 Mannin Beg in his streamlined MG Magnette, known as "the humbug" due to its colour scheme. He is followed at the foot of Bray Hill by Hugh Hamilton's Magnette.

© Lily Publications 2013

Produced and designed by Lily Publications Ltd

Published by: Lily Publications, PO Box 33, Ramsey, Isle of Man IM99 4LP

Tel: +44 (0) 1624 898446   Fax: +44 (0) 1624 898449   E-mail: info@lilypublications.co.uk   Website: www.lilypublications.co.ukPrinte

2

Contents

The author wishes to dedicate this publication to Linda and Robert Kelly, in heartfelt appreciation of all their help, support and encouragement.

The publisher and author would like to thank the following for all their help with this title: R and L Kelly Collection, Charles Guard (Manx Heritage Foundation), Tim Keig, Nicola Cowsill and Bill Snelling (FoTTofinders)

Left: In the 1953 race Stirling Moss made the best of a 1952 works Jaguar 'C' type, lacking the latest modifications, which meant that he had to fight with Hans Ruesch for third place rather than with Reg Parnell for the lead. He had to settle for fourth.

Setting the Scene

Seen at Hillberry in his first motor race, Graeme Fenton was second of th[e] two finishers in the 1907 Heavy Touring Car Race. He was lucky to finish

The Isle of Man is well-known throughout the world for its Tourist Trophy (TT) motorcycle races. Much less well-known, even on the Island, is the fact that there was another TT, for cars, and that the car TT pre-dated the motorcycle races.

In 1904 the Automobile Club of Great Britain and Ireland (which later became the Royal Automobile Club) needed to find a course to hold trials to select a British team to compete in the Gordon Bennett Cup, a car race for national teams held annually in different countries. No suitable course was available in Great Britain as the law did not allow the closure of public roads for motor racing. However Julian Orde, Secretary of the Automobile Club, was a cousin of the Lieutenant-Governor of the Isle of Man, Lord Raglan, and Orde asked his cousin whether a law could be passed on the Isle of Man to allow closure of the Island's roads for the trials. A new law was rushed through Tynwald, the Island's Parliament, in a single day. The trials were held successfully, excited great public interest, and were repeated in 1905. Meanwhile the Auto-Cycle Club, the motor-cycling arm of the Automobile Club, arranged to organise a trial to select a team of racing motorcyclists to represent Great Britain in an international team competition known as the International Cup, a motorcycling version of the Gordon Bennett Cup. This trial was held on the Isle of Man, on the day after the 1905 Gordon Bennett trial but on a shorter course and the first appearance of racing motorcycles on the Isle of Man led directly to the inception of the motorcycle TT in 1907 in the same way as the Gordon Bennett trials led directly to the car TT of 1905.

...rhaps thanks to his monkey mascot, for his Gladiator lost second gear ...tween the finishing line and the enclosure.

At this time the United Kingdom's motor industry was in its infancy, with many manufacturers competing for business. Seeing the interest generated by the Gordon Bennett Trials, Claude Johnson, a partner with the Honourable Charles Rolls and Henry Royce in the Rolls-Royce company, realised the publicity value of a different race, not for the out-and-out racing cars which contested the Gordon Bennett Trials but for "tourist" (touring) cars in which Rolls-Royce and other manufacturers could demonstrate their products to the public in tough competition with those of their rivals. Johnson approached the Automobile Club and Orde asked Lord Raglan for another road closure, in September 1905, for the Tourist Trophy Race. The request was again granted and the first TT race was held in September 1905, over four laps of a course of 52 miles. The race attracted 44 entries of cars of 30 different makes. It was won by John Napier driving an Arrol-Johnston, at an average speed of 33.9 mph. In 1906 the course was reduced to 40.25 miles and the winner was Charles Rolls, driving one of the first Rolls-Royces, averaging 39.6 mph. Then there was pressure for a TT race for motorcycles, resulting in the first motorcycle TT, over the 15.8 miles St. Johns circuit, in 1907. The car TT was also held again in 1907, with classes for "Heavy" and "Light" touring cars which were won by Ernest Courtis (Rover) and George Mills (Beeston-Humber) respectively, at averages of 28.8 mph and 28.1 mph, but criticism of the complicated technical regulations led to a major change for 1908.

The first three TT Races had been based on a complicated formula which placed great emphasis on

Some of the Famous Racers on the Isle of Man

Left: Brian Lewis won all three Mannin Moar Races in 1933, 1934 and 1935. In this 1934 picture he is seated in the 1933 Alfa Romeo Grand Prix car hired for the Isle of Man race from the Scuderia Ferrari. The prancing horse Ferrari badge is prominent on the car's bonnet.

Below: A newcomer to the course, Mike Hawthorn drove with typical determination in the 1952 British Empire Trophy race, finishing third overall and winner of the 1,501cc to 3,000cc class in the smart Frazer Nash Mille Miglia Replica. He lost his life in a road accident in January 1959, soon after winning the 1958 World Championship.

Top: The 1952 British Empire Trophy was one of the motorcycle World Champion and TT winner Geoff Duke's few races for the Aston Martin team during the 1952 season. In a spirited and exciting drive he made the best of a poorly prepared car which was unworthy of his great talent, before retiring with engine failure.

Right: Stirling Moss in 1953, like Geoff Duke in 1952, deserved a better car but made the best of what he was given. The 1952 Jaguar 'C' Type was unable to compete with winner Reg Parnell's Aston Martin DB3S and Moss could manage only fourth, behind Ken Wharton's Frazer Nash and Hans Ruesch's Ferrari.

fuel economy rather than speed alone. Now it was time for an unrestricted race in which speed and durability would be the criteria. The new TT Race became known as the "Four Inch" race because the only restrictions were a minimum weight of 1,600 lb and a maximum of four cylinders with maximum bore diameter of four inches. There was also a new course of 37.5 miles, which followed a route almost identical to today's TT Mountain Course. The difference was that the 1908 car circuit turned right at Cronk-ny-Mona and continued via Johnny Watterson's Lane and Ballanard Road to re-join the later route at the top of Bray Hill. Despite English Press predictions of great danger and serious accidents due to the increased power and higher speeds of cars which more resembled racing rather than touring cars – the Isle of Man was even dubbed "Isle of Manslaughter" – the race was run safely and successfully. The winner was William Watson, driving a Hutton (a modified Napier), at an average speed of 50.25 mph for the nine laps.

The car TT then went into abeyance until its revival in 1914, when it was run over two days with eight laps on each day. The winner was Kenelm Lee Guinness who averaged 56.44 mph in his Sunbeam. After another gap, due to the First World War, the final Isle of Man car TT was held in 1922 over eight laps of an altered course of 37.75 miles, which turned left at Cronk-ny-Mona and followed the present route via Signpost Corner and Governor's Bridge to a start/finish in Glencrutchery Road, near to the present Grandstand. In appallingly wet and muddy conditions, the winner was Jean Chassagne in a Sunbeam, at an average of 55.78 mph. Algernon Lee Guinness won the 1,500cc class in a Talbot Darracq at 53.20 mph and the Bentley team finished

2nd, 4th and 5th, winning the Team Award. There was then another gap until 1928, when the R.A.C decided to revive the race but resolved that the Isle of Man circuit was no longer suitable for the speeds of modern cars. Despite great efforts by the Isle of Man authorities to retain the race on a new circuit, the R.A.C decided to transfer it to the 13.66 miles Ards Circuit in Northern Ireland, causing great disappointment on the Isle of Man.

Another attempt to secure a return to the Island failed in 1930 but resulted in the R.A.C offering the Isle of Man the consolation of "Round the Houses" races in Douglas, modelled on the Monaco Grand Prix. Initially there were two races (the Mannin Beg for small cars and the Mannin Moar for large cars) on Douglas street circuits in 1933, 1934 and 1935. The disruption of road closures in the centre of Douglas caused opposition in 1933, when there was a race of 50 laps (230 miles) on a circuit of 4.6 miles. A shorter circuit of 3.65 miles, avoiding the centre of Douglas, was used in 1934, giving a race length of 182.9 miles. This circuit was used again in 1935, with a minor extension to 4.04 miles and a longer race of 201.75 miles. Brian Lewis (Alfa Romeo) won all three Mannin Moar races while the Mannin Beg winners were Freddie Dixon (Riley), Norman Black (MG) and Pat Fairfield (E.R.A.). For 1936 and 1937 the Mannin Races were dropped in favour of a single 200 miles race called the R.A.C. International Light Car Race. The 1936 race took place on a new four miles circuit on the outskirts of Douglas and through Onchan Village, starting and finishing at the TT Grandstand. The winner was Richard Seaman (Delage). There was yet another change for 1937, with a 3.9 miles circuit which started at the TT Grandstand but turned left at St.

Ninians to swoop down to the Promenade, turning left at the foot of Broadway and continuing along the Promenade to Port Jack before returning via Royal Avenue and Onchan Village to the Grandstand. This race, run over 50 laps (195 miles) in continuous heavy rain, was won by Prince Bira of Siam, driving an E.R.A. The Island authorities then abandoned "Round-the-Houses" races on the grounds that they were not worthwhile but continued negotiations with the R.A.C. to recover the TT Races.

After the Second World War, the major pre-war English circuits, Brooklands, Donington Park and Crystal Palace, were no longer available and proper racing was confined to disused airfields. The British Racing Drivers' Club therefore approached the Isle of Man Government with a proposal to organise its British Empire Trophy race on the 1936 Douglas circuit. Eager to attract tourists, the Government agreed to provide financial and practical support and the first race of this new series was held in August 1947. The British Empire Trophy race was for Formula One racing cars, while there was a support race, the Manx Cup, for smaller cars. The winner of the Empire Trophy was Bob Gerard (E.R.A.) while Prince Bira made a welcome return to the Island to win the Manx Cup in a Simca-Gordini. In 1948 the Empire Trophy was won by Geoff Ansell (E.R.A.), with George Nixon (Riley) winning the Manx Cup. There was a third race, run concurrently with the Manx Cup and called the Castletown Trophy. This race, for racing cars of unlimited engine size, was won by Kenneth Bear in a pre-war Grand Prix Bugatti but was dropped for 1949, when Bob Gerard again won the Empire Trophy and John Heath (H.W.M.-Alta) won the Manx Cup. The 1949 Manx Cup saw the sensational

debut of the 19 years old Stirling Moss, driving a Cooper-J.A.P. Moss was incredibly fast, both in practice and race, and would have won comfortably but for mechanical trouble. The 1950 Empire Trophy, the last for Formula One cars, provided Bob Gerard with his third Isle of Man win, while Oscar Moore won the Manx Cup in his home-build B.M.W. based special.

For 1951 the Empire Trophy race was re-launched as a handicap race for Production Sports Cars. This change was due to the increasing expense and reducing availability of Formula One cars and the increasing popularity of Production Car racing. The winner was Stirling Moss, driving a two litre Frazer Nash, while the last Manx Cup winner was Gerry Dunham in a pre-war Alvis. The Castletown Trophy, revived to cater for larger racing cars no longer eligible for the Empire Trophy but very poorly supported, was won by Reg Parnell in his Maserati.

Pat Griffith had been very unlucky not to win the 1951 Empire Trophy, when a last lap engine failure handed the win to Stirling Moss. Griffith had made the most of his handicap advantage and despite a determined chase Moss could not have caught him. In 1952, Griffith made amends by taking the win but he also was a lucky winner as he would have been caught by world motorcycle racing champion Geoff Duke whose fantastic speed had provided a spectacular race until his Aston Martin stopped with engine failure. He had the consolation of setting a new lap record for sports cars with a lap of 3 minutes 18 seconds (70.53mph).

By 1952 there were growing doubts in Government circles about the value of the races as an attraction to visitors and it had been made clear that the future of the event was on trial. A decision was made to continue for 1953 but it was clear that without a substantial improvement in visitor numbers there would be no event in 1954. The 1953 entry was much improved in numbers and quality. The format of the event was also improved, with the entry of 48 being accommodated in three heats of 16 cars each and a final for 30 cars, which provided spectators with four short, easy to follow races rather than one long race, which could become boring towards the end. The winner was Reg Parnell, driving a works Aston Martin. His fastest lap of 3

minutes 8 seconds (75.48mph) broke his own outright lap record, set in 1950 in a Formula One Maserati, by three seconds and Geoff Duke's 1952 Production Sports Car record by a staggering 13 seconds.

Despite the improvement the 1953 race was to be the last. Deciding that there was insufficient improvement in visitor numbers, the Government abandoned its support for the car races although continuing its attempts to persuade the R.A.C. to agree to the revival of the car TT over the Mountain Course.

The Honourable Brian Lewis won all three Mannin Moar races in 1933, 1934 and 1935. In 1934 he drove a "works" car, borrowed from the Scuderia Ferrari which was running the Alfa Romeo Grand Prix team at the time, and attended by two Ferrari mechanics. Here he is seen at the foot of Broadway, checking rear tyre wear.

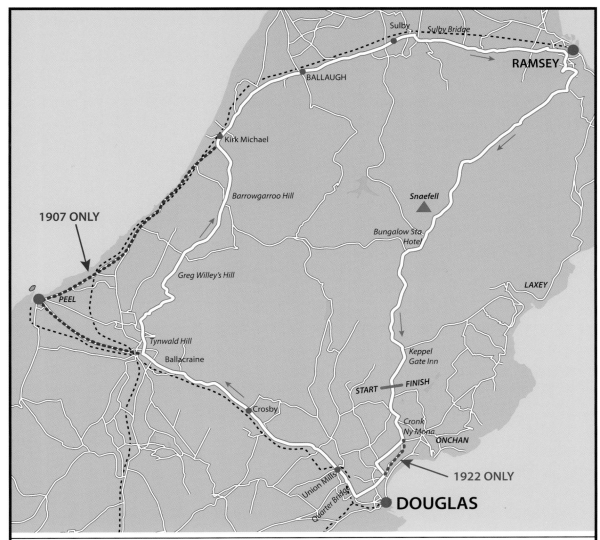

Sulby
Sulby Bridge
RAMSEY
BALLAUGH
Kirk Michael
Barrowgarroo Hill
Snaefell
Bungalow Sta.
Hotel
1907 ONLY
Greg Willey's Hill
LAXEY
PEEL
Tynwald Hill
Ballacraine
Keppel
Gate Inn
START   FINISH
Crosby
Cronk
Ny Mona
ONCHAN
1922 ONLY
Union Mills
Quarter Bridge
DOUGLAS

RAC INTERNATIONAL TOURIST TROPHY RACES 1907, 1914 & 1922

1907 Circuit - 40.25 miles · Lap Record - (1906) Hon. Charles Rolls (Rolls-Royce) 1hr 0mins 13.6sec (39.90mph)
1914 Circuit - 37.50 miles · Lap Record - K. Lee Guinness (Sunbeam) 37mins 56.6sec (59.30mph)
1922 Circuit - 37.75 miles · Lap Record - H.O.D. Segrave (Sunbeam) 39mins 15.2sec (57.70mph)

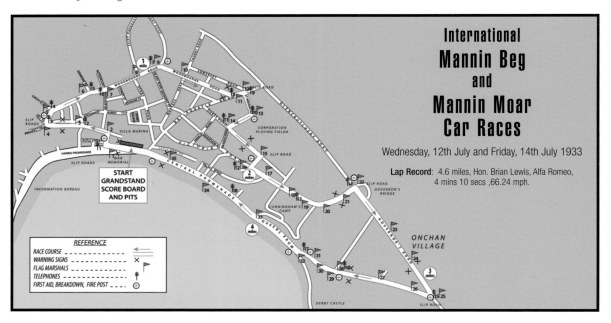

International
Mannin Beg
and
Mannin Moar
Car Races

Wednesday, 12th July and Friday, 14th July 1933

Lap Record: 4.6 miles, Hon. Brian Lewis, Alfa Romeo, 4 mins 10 secs, 66.24 mph.

REFERENCE
RACE COURSE – – – – – – – – –
WARNING SIGNS – – – – – – – – –
FLAG MARSHALS – – – – – – – – –
TELEPHONES – – – – – – – – –
FIRST AID, BREAKDOWN, FIRE POST – – . – .

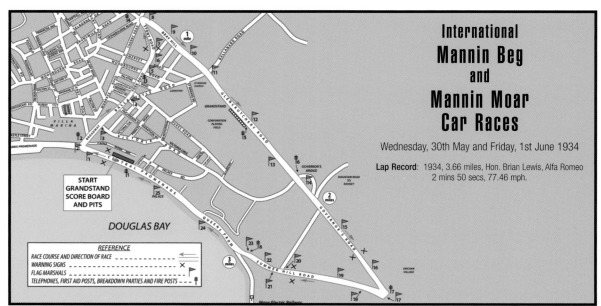

International
Mannin Beg
and
Mannin Moar
Car Races

Wednesday, 30th May and Friday, 1st June 1934

Lap Record: 1934, 3.66 miles, Hon. Brian Lewis, Alfa Romeo, 2 mins 50 secs, 77.46 mph.

REFERENCE
RACE COURSE AND DIRECTION OF RACE – – – – – – – –
WARNING SIGNS – – – – – – – – – – – – – – –
FLAG MARSHALS – – – – – – – – – – – – – – –
TELEPHONES, FIRST AID POSTS, BREAKDOWN PARTIES AND FIRE POSTS – – –

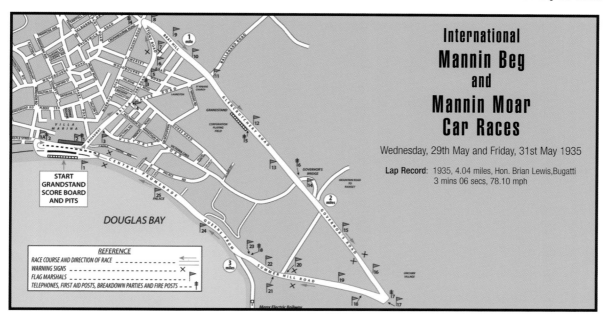

International
Mannin Beg
and
Mannin Moar
Car Races

Wednesday, 29th May and Friday, 31st May 1935

Lap Record: 1935, 4.04 miles, Hon. Brian Lewis, Bugatti
3 mins 06 secs, 78.10 mph

REFERENCE

RACE COURSE AND DIRECTION OF RACE ⸺ ⸺ ⸺
WARNING SIGNS ⸺ ⸺ ⸺ ⸺ ⸺ ⸺ ✕
FLAG MARSHALS ⸺ ⸺ ⸺ ⸺ ⸺ ⸺
TELEPHONES, FIRST AID POSTS, BREAKDOWN PARTIES AND FIRE POSTS ⸺ ⸺ ⸺

START GRANDSTAND SCORE BOARD AND PITS

DOUGLAS BAY

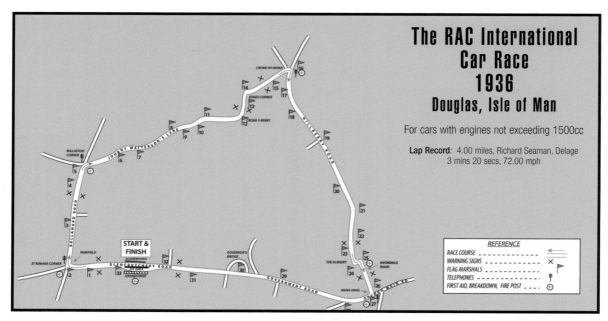

The RAC International
Car Race
1936
Douglas, Isle of Man

For cars with engines not exceeding 1500cc

Lap Record: 4.00 miles, Richard Seaman, Delage
3 mins 20 secs, 72.00 mph

REFERENCE

RACE COURSE ⸺ ⸺ ⸺ ⸺ ⸺
WARNING SIGNS ⸺ ⸺ ⸺ ⸺ ✕
FLAG MARSHALS ⸺ ⸺ ⸺ ⸺
TELEPHONES ⸺ ⸺ ⸺ ⸺ ⸺
FIRST AID, BREAKDOWN, FIRE POST ⸺ ⸺ ⊕

START & FINISH

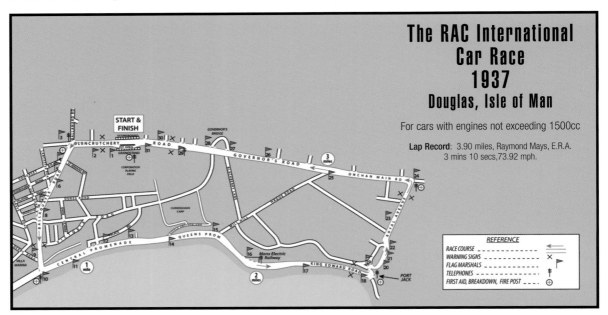

The RAC International Car Race 1937

Douglas, Isle of Man

For cars with engines not exceeding 1500cc

Lap Record: 3.90 miles, Raymond Mays, E.R.A.
3 mins 10 secs, 73.92 mph.

REFERENCE

RACE COURSE
WARNING SIGNS
FLAG MARSHALS
TELEPHONES
FIRST AID, BREAKDOWN, FIRE POST

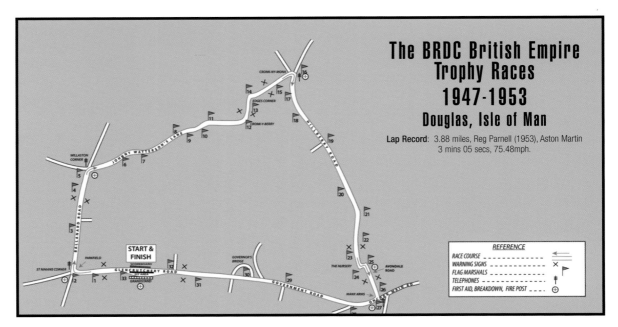

The BRDC British Empire Trophy Races 1947-1953

Douglas, Isle of Man

Lap Record: 3.88 miles, Reg Parnell (1953), Aston Martin
3 mins 05 secs, 75.48mph.

REFERENCE

RACE COURSE
WARNING SIGNS
FLAG MARSHALS
TELEPHONES
FIRST AID, BREAKDOWN, FIRE POST

Frank Clement's 1914 TT ended on lap 10 with a broken piston in his Straker-Squire's engine. During the event, however, he met W.O. Bentley who was driving his own D.F.P. and this meeting led to Clement driving in the winning Bentley team in the 1922 TT. Clement finished second to Jean Chassagne's Sunbeam in that race.

The winner of the 1914 TT, held over two days and sixteen laps, Kenelm Lee Guinness driving a Sunbeam led at the end of the first day and dominated the second day, beating the second-placed Minerva of C. Riecken by just under twenty minutes.

Kenelm Lee Guinness' elder brother, Algernon, driving a Sunbeam was placed second to Kenelm at the end of the first day in 1914 but retired on lap 13 with transmission failure after struggling with brake problems. He won the 1,500cc class in the 1922 TT, driving a Talbot-Darracq.

J. PORPORATO "MINERVA"

One of the Belgian Minerva team which won the team prize, Jean Porporato finished fifth. The other team cars of Riecken and Molon finished second and third respectively. The team caused controversy during practising due to the smoke-screens caused by their sleeve-valve engines but pre-race adjustments did little to cure the problem.

William Watson, the 1908 TT winner in a Hutton, is seen here at Quarterbridge in his Vauxhall awaiting the start of a morning practice session in 1914. He was much less fortunate in 1914 than in 1908, retiring at Union Mills, only two miles into the first lap, with a broken crankshaft.

M. CHASSAGNE "SUNBEAM"

Jean Chassagne ran second to Segrave in another Sunbeam for the first three laps, taking the lead when Segrave was delayed by a puncture. He then led to the end, averaging over 55 mph in appalling conditions and beating Frank Clement, who had been delayed behind a 1,500cc Bugatti, by four minutes.

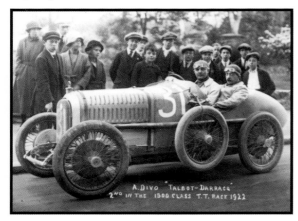

A. DIVO "TALBOT-DARRACQ" 2ND IN THE 1500 CLASS T.T. RACE 1922

Albert Divo finished second to his team-mate Algernon Lee Guinness in the 1922 TT 1,500cc Trophy Race. The third team member, Jean Morriceau, crashed near Glen Helen when a tyre burst as he tried to overtake Mones Maury's Bugatti.

MONES MAURY "CROSSLEY-BUGATTI"

A Spanish nobleman and a Captain in the Royal Flying Corps during World War 1, the Marquis de Casca Maury (known as Mones Maury) finished third in the 1,500cc race in the 1922 TT, driving one of the winning team of Type 13 Bugattis.

Freddie Dixon, the 1933 Mannin Beg winner in a Riley, was well-known and popular on the Isle of Man due to his motorcycle racing career. He competed in 17 TT races between 1912 and 1928, with wins in the 1921 Sidecar TT on his Douglas outfit and in the 1927 Junior TT on an H.R.D.

Norman Black, the 1934 Mannin Beg winner in an MG Magnette, was a London sports car dealer and former TT motorcycle racer. In 1931 he won the car TT at Ards and the Irish Grand Prix. In 1932 he won the light car class at Le Mans. He was also a successful hill-climb and rally driver.

Norman Black. "M.G. Maquette" Mannin Beg. 1934. Winners of the Race.

1934 Mannin Beg runner-up Charlie Dodson in an MG Magnette was another ex-motorcycle racer. He rode in the TT from 1925 to 1934, with Senior TT wins in 1928 and 1929. He also won two car TT races at Ards, in 1934 in an MG and in 1936, in a Riley shared with Freddie Dixon.

C.J.P. Dodson 2nd in Mannin Moar 1934.

W. L. Handley
"M.G. Magnette" Mc

Walter Handley had a formidable reputation on the Island for his skill, courage and determination in the motorcycle TT, where his forceful riding resulted in four wins. He brought the same qualities to car racing, driving for MG, but retired in his only Island races, the Mannin Beg races of 1934 and 1935.

By the end of the first lap of the Mannin Beg, Walter Handley had forced his way into a substantial lead. Starting the second lap, he approached the right turn off the Promenade into Broadway at a speed far too fast even for him. Sliding sideways with both off-side wheels in the air, he hit and bounced off the sand bags at the foot of the lamp standard in the centre of the road. With his fuel tank holed and rear axle bent, he was forced to retire.

Climbing Broadway on the first lap of the 1934 Mannin Moar, the Bugatti of Tim Rose-Richards leads the pack in pursuit of leader Brian Lewis. Following Rose-Richards are Freddie Dixon (Riley), Charlie Dodson and Vasco Sameiro (Alfa Romeos) and Richard Shuttleworth (Bugatti). Rose-Richards retired on lap 14.

At the start of the 1934 Mannin Moar, Brian Lewis (4) and Freddie Dixon (7) are on the front row, followed by the Bugattis of Rose-Richards (2) and Chris Staniland (1), Sameiro's Alfa Romeo (12), Dodson's Alfa Romeo (9), Shuttleworth's Bugatti (11) and Paul's Riley (8).

Lindsay Eccles drove Bugattis in the three Mannin Moar races, but never finished. Here he spins at the hairpin corner at the south (Greensill's corner) end of the loop which was added to the 1934 circuit for the 1935 race to avoid the right turn into Broadway where Walter Handley crashed in 1934.

In the Mannin Beg, Roy Eccles took over an Alta entered by Alfred Lace, which was to have been driven by D. Tennant. Here the car is seen at the left hand bend from the new loop on the Promenade into Broadway. Eccles retired on lap 4 with a split fuel tank. He finished fifth in the 1934 Mannin Beg, in an MG Magnette.

A protégé of Freddie Dixon, Pat Fairfield had a reputation of an erratic driver in his early career, earning the nickname of "Skidder". His victory in the 1935 Mannin Beg, driving the first E.R.A. to be sold to a customer, was the company's first major success. He was fourth in the 1936 Manx race and third in 1937. He is pictured rounding the Greensill's hairpin.

W. L. Handley. M.G.R. Mannin Beg 1935.

Walter Handley retained his place in the MG team for the 1935 Mannin Beg. He was second fastest in practice, only a second slower than race winner Pat Fairfield, but retired on the third lap with transmission failure. This was his last Isle of Man race.

Manxman Alfred Lace raced in the 1933 Mannin Moar in an Invicta, but retired after crashing into a telegraph pole on Summer Hill. In the 1935 Mannin Beg his luck did not improve. His Alta failed to move from the start line and had to be pushed to his pit. He finally got away but retired after a first lap which took an hour and a half!

Although he drove Alfa Romeos in the 1933 and 1934 Mannin Moar races, Brian Lewis was better known as a Bugatti driver, earning the nickname of "Bug". He returned to a Bugatti for the 1935 race, claiming his hat-trick of Mannin Moar victories. Here, he exits the hairpin.

Pictured at the foot of Broadway, Charlie Martin finished fourth in the 1934 Mannin Beg in an MG Magnette. For 1935, he had a 3.3 litre Grand Prix Bugatti, in which he was runner-up to the similar car of Brian Lewis. The car returned to the Island to win the 1948 Castletown Trophy, driven by Kenneth Bear.

Brian Lewis'Bugatti leads the field round the Greensill's hairpin, followed by Richard Shuttleworth's Alfa Romeo (3), Charlie Martin's Bugatti (10), Lindsay Eccles' Bugatti (9), Luis Fontes' Alfa Romeo (5), Raymond Mays' E.R.A. (15), Tim Rose-Richards' Maserati (6), Charlie Brackenbury's Bugatti (11), E. K. Rayson's Bugatti (16), Humphrey Cook's E.R.A. (14), A.P. Hamilton's Alfa Romeo (1), Wilkins' Alfa Romeo (2), Arthur Dobson's Alfa Romeo (4) and the Hon. Jock Leith's Bugatti (8).

1936

Prince Birabongse Bhanubandh (known as "B. Bira" or "Bira") was a Siamese prince, grandson of King Mongkut on whom the main character in the musical "The King and I" was based. In only his second season of racing Bira, driving an E.R.A., was runner-up to Richard Seaman.

The 1933 Mannin Beg winner retired 17 miles from the finish after leading for 35 laps in 1934 and finished second in 1935 but 1936 was the year when Dixon did not race. After practising his Riley, he said that the circuit was unsuitable for racing and that he was going fishing.

Philip Jucker competed in numerous races during 1936, but with little success. On the Island he retired his Frazer Nash on the third lap with engine failure. Sadly, he was fatally injured when he crashed his Alta at Port Jack during the first morning practice for the 1937 Isle of Man race.

Above: Pictured here at the Manx Arms corner in Oncha[n] ("Dick") Seaman was already a very promising driver whe[n] attracted considerable interest by his decision to race a 1[9] Delage Grand Prix car for the 1936 season. He led the rac[e] the fourth lap until the finish.

Left: Cyril Paul is pictured leading Bira at Willlaston corne[r] driving E.R.A.'s. In 1934, he was sixth in the Mannin Beg in the Mannin Moar, driving Rileys. After a year's absence, returned to the Island in 1936, finishing third behind Sean Bira.

After a fine d[rive] Seaman ackn[owledged] victory in his [Isle] of Man race. [After a] highly succes[sful] season, he jo[ined] Mercedes Be[nz Grand] Prix team for [1937] and remained [with the] team for 193[8 and] 1939 but cra[shed] fatally when l[eading] the 1939 Bel[gian] Grand Prix in [wet] conditions.

Bira arrived with the 1936 winning Delage, pictured here during practice, and an E.R.A. He decided to race the E.R.A. as his best E.R.A. practice time was equal fastest with Raymond Mays, seven seconds faster than his best time in the Delage. Bira won the race, in heavy rain. Mays was the runner-up.

Above: Pat Fairfield is seen turning his E.R.A. out of Broadway onto the Promenade in the very heavy rain which continued throughout the race. He finished third behind Bira and Raymond Mays. Only weeks afterwards, he lost his life in a multiple crash at the Le Mans 24 hour race.

Right: Baron Emanuel ("Toulo") de Graffenried (Maserati) was a Swiss driver who took up racing in 1936 and continued until 1955. He finished sixth, one lap short of the full race distance. He won the 1949 British Grand Prix at Silverstone.

1937

33

34

One of the partners in the E.R.A. company, Raymond Mays drove one of the cars in the Mannin Beg and Mannin Moar of 1935 and in the 1936 race, retiring each time, but finished second to Bira in the rain-soaked 1937 race.

Driving an old and unreliable MG in his Island debut race, Reg Parnell was the twelfth and last finisher, completing only 35 of the 50 laps after many pit stops. His post-war Isle of Man races also attracted much bad luck, but ultimate success.

Luigi Villoresi, who retired his Maserati on lap 15 of the Manx race, was one of the most successful Italian drivers of the thirties, with numerous wins in Europe and in South Africa. He also won the first post-war British Grand Prix at Silverstone in 1948.

1947

Above: George Abecassis and John Heath founded H.W. Motors and produced H.W.-Alta and H.W.M. racing cars. Both also raced in the early post-war years. In 1947, Abecassis raced a streamlined "A" type E.R.A. but retired in the British Empire Trophy race after a crash in Onchan caused by loss of vision after an oil pipe burst.

Right: Bira returned to the Island with a "works" Simca Gordini, ten years after his first Manx victory, to win the Manx Cup race. He is pictured at the Manx Arms corner at the junction of Main Road and Avondale Road in Onchan Village.

Fastest in practice for both races, Bira was fancied as a potential double winner. After four pit stops in the first six laps of the British Empire Trophy race due to various problems with his Maserati, he did well to finish fifth, two laps behind the winner, Bob Gerard.

Pictured at Parkfield driving a new "E" type E.R.A. which had been de-tuned for reliability in what was regarded as an experimental race, Leslie Brooke drove well to finish fourth in the Empire Trophy race. It was the first finish for this new car in an international race.

The 1947 Empire Trophy race was Sheila Darbishire's only Isle of Man race. She finished eight and next to last in her Riley. She practised for the 1948 Empire Trophy but was a non-starter after engine trouble in the final practice.

Bob Gerard was the most successful driver in the seven Empire Trophy races held on the Isle of Man, with three wins, one second and one retirement in the five races in which he competed. Illustrated at the Manx Arms in his E.R.A., 1947 was the first of his victories.

Jack Scott was one of the H.R.G team of three cars which won the team prize in the Manx Cup. Scott and Peter Clark drove streamlined cars, finishing seventh and eleventh respectively, while the third conventionally-bodied car of A.C. Molyneux finished twelfth.

Manx Cup race driver Eric Winterbottom is pictured in his 1,100cc supercharged Emeryson. Typical of "specials" produced in the early post-war years, the car was said to have been built from parts of seven different makes, some over 25 years old. He finished third.

A member of the Ansell's Brewery family, Geoff Ansell started racing in 1947, finishing ninth in the Manx Cup, driving an Aston Martin. The British Empire Trophy was only his second race in his E.R.A. He was a lucky winner after Reg Parnell retired on the last lap.

Close to the gate pillars at Parkfield, bare-headed Leslie Brooke in his E.R.A. presses on to a creditable third place in the British Empire Trophy race. He achieved third despite being pushed into the sandbags at Onchan by Bob Ansell when he slowed to let Ansell overtake!

A noted Bugatti enthusiast, Kenneth Bear won the Castletown Trophy race in the 1933 Grand Prix Bugatti in which Charlie Martin finished second in the 1935 Mannin Moar. Bear crashed the car fatally in the 1949 Jersey road race.

Derek Buckler specialized in constructing chassis for builders of "specials" and competed in his own cars in trials and races. He finished twelfth and last in the Manx Cup in a car which was essentially a home-made trials special with a standard Ford Ten engine.

"Curly" Dryden entered an early 500cc Cooper in the 1948 Manx Cup but unfortunately over-turned it in practice on the left-hand bend at Cronk-y-Berry. He was pinned under the car but escaped with cuts and bruises. He was a non-starter in the race.

The Hector Graham/D.H. Kyle MG is pictured facing the wrong way at Parkfield after a spin. The car ran out of fuel less than three laps from the end of the Manx Cup race.

Guy Jason-Henry spun his Delahaye on melting tar at Parkfield during the British Empire Trophy race. He restarted and finished seventh. He finished twelfth in the 1949 race.

Manx Cup winner George Nixon rounds Parkfield in his first road race. His car was a "special" with a Riley engine owned by Freddie Dixon. He had serious engine problems in the first practice and was running-in his engine in the second practice and early in the race.

After serious problems during practice which meant a great deal of frantic work, French driver Maurice Monnier crashed his Monnier Special at Willaston corner on the second lap of the Manx Cup race. A bent front axle forced his retirement.

Reg Parnell led for most of the Empire Trophy race. As he started the last lap with a lead of more than a lap, he switched to his reserve fuel tank and his Maserati's engine spluttered and died. As he tried to restore the flow of fuel, Geoff Ansell passed him to take a lucky victory.

Dennis Poore was fastest in practice for the Castletown Trophy race but was delayed early in the race when his Alfa Romeo's radiator cap opened and drenched him with hot water and steam. Despite doing the fastest lap, he was unable to catch the winner, Kenneth Bear, and finished second.

On his first visit to the Island, Roy Salvadori is pictured at the Manx Arms in his British Empire Trophy Maserati. He retired with valve problems. In the Castletown Trophy race, he was delayed by stops for plug changes before retiring with broken valve springs.

In his only Isle of Man race, D.A. Wilcocks retired his supercharged MG Midget on lap 9 of the Manx Cup race with lubrication problems. He is pictured spinning at Parkfield.

Above: George Abecassis entered the Grand Prix Alta for the 1949 British Empire Trophy but John Heath took it over after Abecassis was injured in a practice crash in their Manx Cup Cooper. Heath (pictured second from left) finished tenth but won the Manx Cup in an H.W.-Alta.

Left: Belgian driver and jazz band leader Johnny Claes drove a Talbot-Lago to eighth place in his only British Empire Trophy race. He was also a successful rally driver, twice winning the Liege-Rome-Liege classic.

After an unsuccessful drive in 1948 in an H.R.G., Dudley Folland had a two litre Ferrari 166 for the 1949 Manx Cup race. After a strong drive, challenging Stirling Moss and John Heath for the lead, he retired with clutch failure after nine laps.

After retiring in the 1948 British Empire Trophy race, Bob Gerard secured his second win in the 1949 event with his E.R.A. after early leader Reg Parnell retired and Fred Ashmore, who took over the lead, was delayed after an impact while overtaking another car.

The 1949 Manx Cup winner stands by his H.W. Alta near the start/finish line. Starting from the third row of the grid, John Heath was third after five laps, took the lead after Folland retired and was a surprise winner when Stirling Moss retired three laps from the finish.

Stirling Moss, 19 years old and racing outside England for the first time, was the sensation of the event. Fastest by five seconds in his Cooper in practice for the Manx Cup, he led the race from the start until three laps from the end, when he retired with slipped magneto drive.

David Murray takes Parkfield in his Maserati. He retired in the British Empire Trophy in 1949, 1950 and 1952 but was runner-up to Reg Parnell in the 1951 Castletown Trophy race.

Bob Gerard was again unbeatable in the 1950 British Empire Trophy in his E.R.A., claiming his third win in four races. He avoided trouble when others slid on slippery roads in the early laps, making only one mistake when he lost the lead briefly after over-shooting at Parkfield.

Baron Emanuel de Graffenried, who finished sixth in the 1937 race, arrived late for the 1950 British Empire Trophy, missing the first practice. For the second practice, he shared his Maserati with Bira, whose car had not arrived. Nevertheless, he qualified and finished third in the race.

Driving his O.B.M., a B.M.W. engined special developed from the Frazer Nash B.M.W. which he had raced in 1947, Oscar Moore won the Manx Cup after the Coopers of Eric Brandon, John Cooper and Hector Graham, which had dominated the early laps, dropped out one by one.

Above: "Spike" Rhiando from the U.S.A., who entered Coopers in the 1948 and 1949 Manx Cup races, retiring in 1948 and non-starting in 1949, returned in 1950 with his Rhiando-Trimax but his bad luck continued when he retired on the first lap.

Below: Peter Walker drove in the 1937 Manx race and returned in 1948, 1949 and 1950. During practice for the 1950 British Empire Trophy he crashed his "E" type E.R.A. at Cronk-y-Berry. The car caught fire and Walker was hospitalised with rib and wrist injuries.

Wearing a helmet with the Manx three legs emblem, Isle of Man resident Bill Murray drove his H.R.G. in the 1950 Manx Cup, crashing at Parkfield on the third lap. He entered a Frazer Nash for the 1951 British Empire Trophy but retired in a multiple crash on the first lap.

Reg Parnell's bad luck continued. Troubled from lap 3 of the Empire Trophy race by an intermittentl1 slipping clutch, he led for a short time but could finish only sixth. He had the consolation of setting a new lap record three laps from the end.

Geoff Duke, who had won three TT races and two World Championships on two wheels, tried racing on four wheels with a Aston Martin DB3 during the 1952 season. He was second fastest in practice but, in the race, was slowed by an electrical problem while fourth on handicap. He later retired with engine failure.

Stationary against the sandbags at Parkfield, Stanley Boshier in his Jaguar XK 120 watches as Roy Salvadori passes in his Frazer Nash. Boshier re-joined the race and finished eleventh, while Salvadori finished fourth and second in his class.

Mike Llewellyn's almost completely standard MG TD emphasised that the 1952 British Empire Trophy was a production car race. In his only race on the Isle of Man he finished a creditable ninth, only three seconds behind the similar car of Trevor Line.

Cliff Davis raced this Cooper MG, with a body resembling a miniature Ferrari, in the 1952 and 1953 British Empire Trophy races. In 1952 he retired with bearing trouble. In 1953 he won his heat but retired in the final with a broken half-shaft.

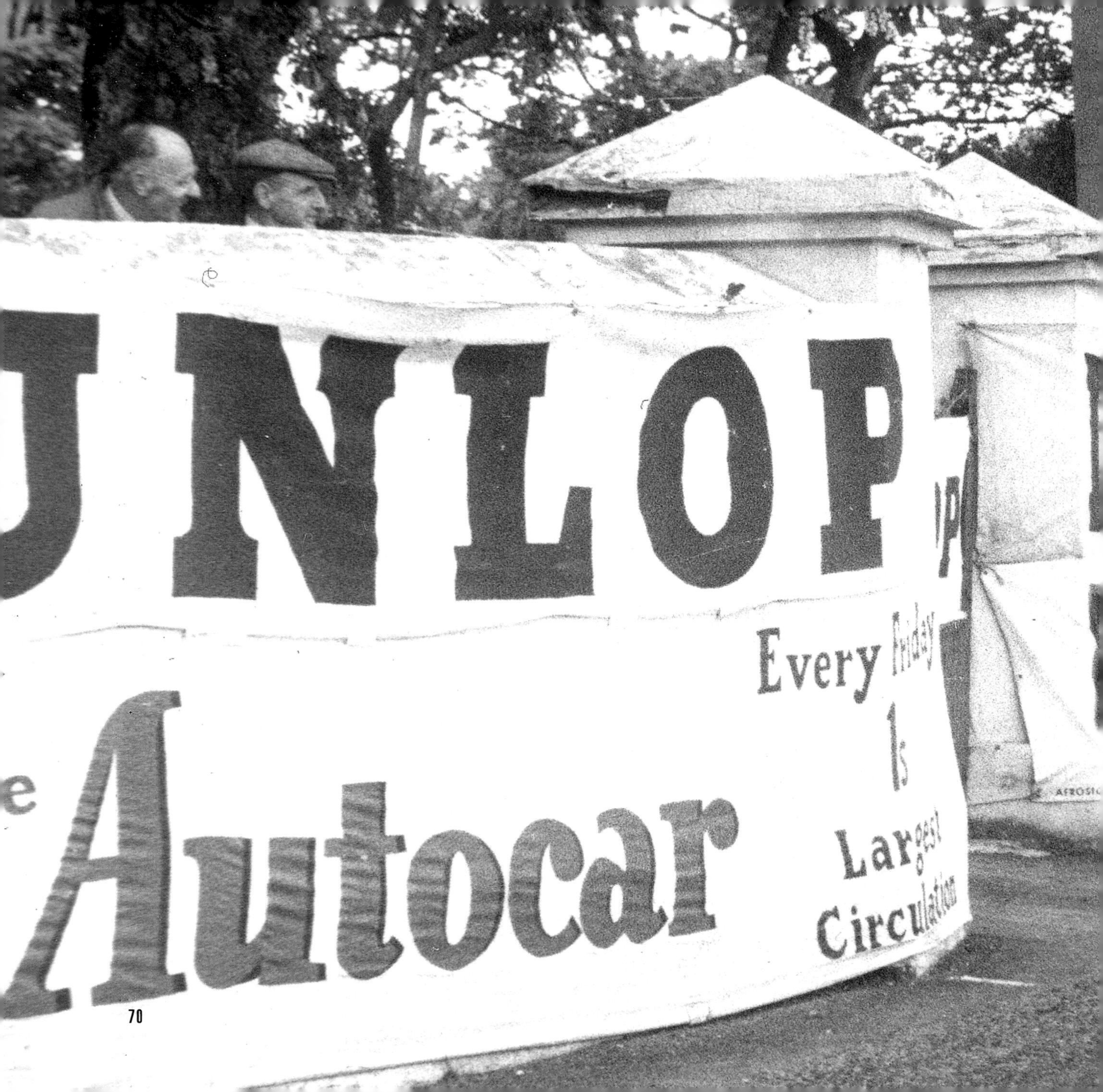
UNLOP
e Autocar
Every Friday
1s
Largest
Circulation

Race winner Pat Griffith had been unlucky not to win in 1951, when his last lap retirement let Stirling Moss take a fortunate win. In 1952, Griffith's luck changed, although Geoff Duke could well have caught him if his Aston Martin had been reliable.

Duncan Hamilton started from pole position and led the field into Parkfield on the first lap, followed by Hawthorn, Salvadori, Duke and Mitchell. Hamilton's "C" type Jaguar was reputedly the only one in private hands. He retired with rear axle failure.

Mike Hawthorn drove the only Mille Miglia replica Frazer Nash in the race, the others being the Le Mans model. He finished third and won his class in his only Island race. He went on to become World Champion in 1958.

Lionel Leonard finished 12th in his Cooper MG in 1951. He retired from the 1952 race with a blown gasket but, in 1953, he was 5th in his heat and 11th in the final in the more streamlined Leonard MG.

Overleaf: Driving the Le Mans replica Frazer Nash in which he had won the 1951 British Empire Trophy, Stirling Moss had a very troublesome race, with numerous pit stops. He eventually retired with electrical and fuel feed problems.

Left: The Jowett Jupiter was the sports version of the Jowett Javelin saloon. Both were popular and successful racing and rally cars from 1949 to 1952. Five were entered, of which three started. Two finished, seventh and tenth, but Bill Skelly retired with valve trouble.

Above: Alfred Hitchings' Cadillac Allard was the only non-Jaguar among the nine cars in the over three litres class. He retired with gearbox trouble. For the 1953 race, he changed to a Lester MG and finished eighth in his heat and sixteenth in the final.

Previous page: Sir James Scott Douglas was a member of the Ecurie Ecosse team, with David Murray and Ian Stewart. He was the first Jaguar driver to finish, in sixth place.

In his streamlined "flying saucer" Golding-Cooper with a two litre Bristol engine, John Barber finished seventh in his heat, but retired in the final. He had previously raced on the Island in the 1951 Manx Cup, when he also retired.

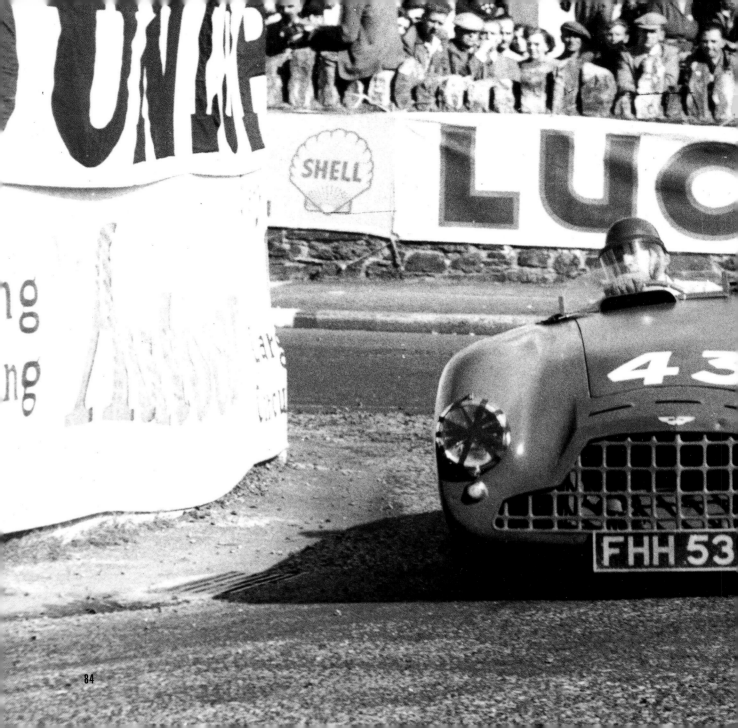

1953

2

85

Alan Brown in his smart Cooper-Bristol was placed second to Ken Wharton in his heat after both had broken the lap record twice. In the final, he retired with a blown cylinder head gasket after running second to Ken Wharton for four laps.

Previous page: In his only Manx event, Bob Dickson drove his three litre Aston Martin to seventh place in his heat and eleventh in the final. His was the only Aston Martin to finish, apart from Reg Parnell's DB3S.

Above: Horace Gould raced an un-streamlined Cooper MG, in which he retired in his heat at Cronk-ny-Mona, with engine trouble. It was his only Manx race.

Starting from the second row of the grid, Ernest Harewood stormed past Davis' Cooper and the Kiefts of Mayers and Griffith to lead the field through Parkfield in his elderly MG. He soon lost the lead, later re-gained it, but retired on lap 9 with gearbox trouble.

The 1953 Aston Martin DB3S was a much better car than the DB3 driven by Geoff Duke in 1952. Making the most of the car, Reg Parnell comfortably won both his heat and the final, at last deservedly claiming the British Empire Trophy victory which had been so elusive.

Swiss driver Hans Ruesch had many successes between 1933 and 1939, including victory in the 1936 Donington Grand Prix in an Alfa Romeo shared with Richard Seaman. Pictured at Parkfield in his Ferrari 340, pursued by Stirling Moss, Ruesch was third in his heat and third in the final.

Above: Another streamlined Cooper, the Cornhill Racing Team Cooper-Riley driven by John Riseley-Pritchard had engine problems during practice and was a non-starter in its heat.

Left: Peter Scott-Russell spent both the heat and the final scrapping with Gerry Dunham, driving a similar Frazer Nash. In the heat, Scott-Russell finished fourth, beating Dunham by one second but in the final Dunham turned the tables, finishing seventh and beating Scott-Russell by two seconds. They were second and third in class.

Four times British hill-climb champion, Ken Wharton was also a proficient trials, rally and circuit racing driver. He raced only once on the Island, in a Frazer Nash. He won his heat and finished second in the final, 18 seconds behind Reg Parnell and 37 seconds ahead of Hans Ruesch.

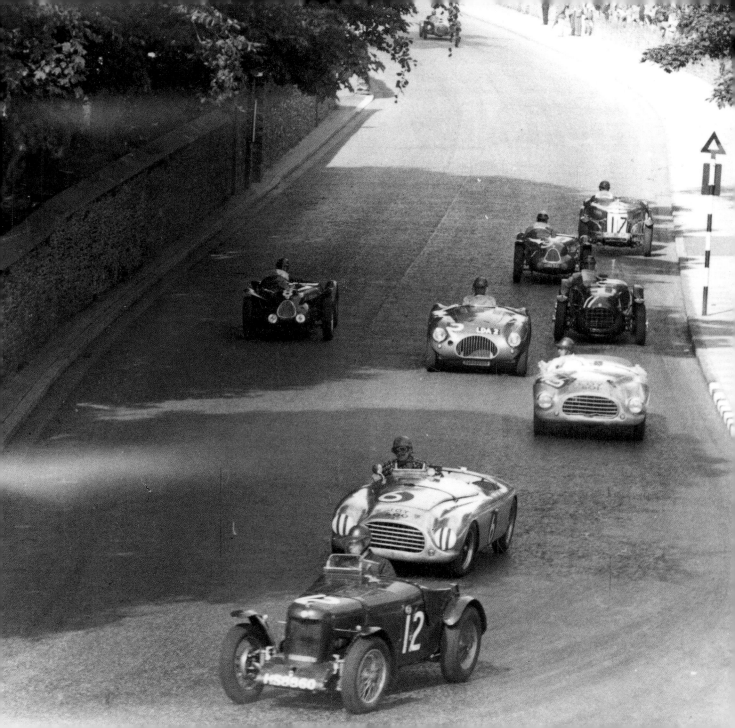

Above: Elder brother of Sir Jackie, Jimmy Stewart drove one of three Ecurie Ecosse Jaguar "C" types in his only Isle of Man race. He finished fifth in his heat and sixth in the final, five seconds behind team mate Ninian Sanderson. The other team driver, Ian Stewart (no relation), retired in his heat.

Left: At Parkfield, Harewood's MG (12) leads from Cliff Davis' Cooper-MG (6), Lionel Leonard's Leonard-MG (15), Pat Griffith's Kieft (2), Alfred Hitchings' Cooper-MG (8) John Haesendonck's MG (11), Peter Jackson's Lester MG (9), Ted Lund's MG (17) and Chris Threlfall's Tojeiro (14).

More about
TT racing on the Isle of Ma

Over the last 20 years Lily Publications has produced some of the most definitive boc
on this most famous of racecourses, and we have even more titles in the pipeline...

Manx Car Races – The Golden Years 1904-1953, Volume 1 96 pages, price £16.00

Published in May 2013 and written by Neil Hanson – a local Manx author who has followed car racing on the Island for
years. This book begins with a short historical account of car racing on the Isle of Man from 1904 and leads into a wide
selection of historical pictures from R & L Kelly collection and that of the Keig family photographic business. Maps and c
information are included to help the reader bring these stunning images to life.

Isle of Man TT – The Golden Years 1907-1939 96 pages, price £16.00

This book captures a wealth of Isle of Man historical motorcycle racing views from island photographers Keig Photograp
Many photos in this book have never been published and the collection of pictures is complemented with detailed capti
written by Mick Duckworth, the renowned Manx motorbike author. Published September/October 2013.

Isle of Man TT Golden Years Series

Three further books in this series will be published by Lily Publications over the next two years. To follow on from the TT
a series of four books will be produced on the Manx Grand Prix, all using pictures from the Keig Photographic collection
See our website for further information on these titles.

Other TT books from Lily Publications...

Realising the Dream at the TT   A4 style, 192 pages, price £15.00

This book celebrates 50 years of road racing on the Isle of Man by Honda. Many previously unpublished pictures are inc
in this book which begins the story in 1959 when the Honda team travelled 6,000 miles from Japan to the Isle of Man.

Shutterspeed   128 pages, price £18.00

This book gives the reader a selection of outstanding pictures taken by local motorcyclist photographer Dave Collister w
complementary text by Manx journalist and writer Mick Duckworth. A must for all TT fans.

For further details or to order any of these titles and many other Isle of Man books visit **www.lilypublication**
or contact: Lily Publications Ltd, PO Box 33, Ramsey, Isle of Man, IM99 4LP Tel: 01624 898446.